Guitar Chord Songbook

Grateful Dead

ISBN 978-1-4950-0698-2

HAL•LEONARD®
CORPORATION
7777 W. BLUEMOUND RD. P.O. BOX 13819 MILWAUKEE, WI 53213

Visit Hal Leonard Online at
www.halleonard.com

Guitar Chord Songbook

Contents

Althea

Words by Robert Hunter
Music by Jerry Garcia

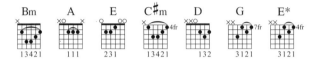

Intro   ‖: Bm   A |E   A | Bm   A |E   :‖

Verse 1
    Bm   A   E   A
I told Al - thea I was feeling lost,

    Bm   A   E
Lacking in some di - rection.

    Bm   A   E   A
Althea told me upon   scrutiny

          Bm   A   E
That my   back might ___ need protec - tion.

Chorus 1
    A   C#m
I told Althea that treachery

    D   A
Was tearin' me limb from limb.

    C#m   E
Althea told me, "Now,   cool down, boy.

    Bm   A   E
Settle back,   easy, Jim."

| Guitar Solo 1 | ‖: Bm   A   \|E   A   \|Bm   A   \|E   :‖ |

Verse 2

Bm   A   E   A
You may be Saturday's child, all grown,

Bm   A   E
Moving with a   pinch of grace.

Bm   A   E   A
You may be a clown in the burying ground,

Bm   A   E
Or just another   pretty face.

Chorus 2

A   C♯m
You may be the fate of O - phelia,

D   A
Sleeping and perchance to dream.

C♯m   E
Honest to the point of recklessness,

Bm   A   E
Self-centered   to the ex - treme.

Guitar Solo 2

Repeat Guitar Solo 1

Verse 3

Bm   A   E   A
Ain't nobody mess - in' with you but you,

Bm   A   E
Your friends are getting most con - cerned.

Bm   A   E   A
Loose with the truth, maybe it's your fire.

Bm   A   E
Baby,   don't get burned.

Chorus 3

A   C♯m
"When the smoke has cleared," she said,

D   A
That's what she said to me.

C♯m   E
"Gonna want a bed   to lay your head

Bm   A   E
And a little   sympa - thy."

Guitar Solo 3　　　*Repeat Guitar Solo 1*

Bridge
```
        D                   G
        There are things you can replace,
        E*
        And others you cannot,
        D                   G
        The time has come to weigh those things,
        E*
        This space is getting hot,
        Bm          A           E
        You know this space is getting hot.
```

Guitar Solo 4　　　*Repeat Guitar Solo 1*

Verse 4
```
        Bm       A     E       A
        I told Al - thea I'm a roving sign,
        Bm            A          E
        That I was born ___ to be a bach - 'lor.
        Bm       A      E      A
        Althea told me, "Okay, ___ that's fine."
        Bm   A                  E
        So now, I'm tryin' to catch ___ her.
```

Chorus 4
```
        A                        C#m
        I can't talk to you without talking to me,
              D                 A
        We're guilty of the same old thing,
        C#m              E
        Thinking a lot about    less and less,
        Bm           A          E
        And forgetting    the love we bring.
```

Outro-Guitar Solo　　　*Repeat Guitar Solo 1 and fade*

Brokedown Palace

Words by Robert Hunter
Music by Jerry Garcia

Melody:

Fare you _ well, my _ hon-ey.

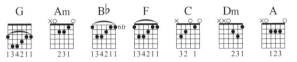

Intro | G | | | | | |

Prelude
          G   Am
       Fare you well, my honey.

          B♭   F   C
       Fare you well, my only true one.

          G   Dm
       All the birds that were singing

           B♭   C   F
       Are flown except you a - lone.

Verse 1
           F   B♭
       Goin' to leave this brokedown palace,

              F   Dm
       On my hands and my knees.

            B♭   F
       I will roll, roll, roll.

                      Am   B♭   F
       Make myself a bed ___ by the waterside,

                       G
       In my time, in my time,

            B♭   F
       I will roll, roll, roll.

Chorus 1   **F**   **A**
In a bed, in a bed,

     B♭   **F**   **G**
By the waterside I will lay my head.

F   **G**
Listen to the river sing ____ sweet songs

 B♭   **F**
To rock my soul.

Verse 2   **F**   **B♭**
River goin' to take me, sing me sweet and sleepy.

F   **Dm**   **B♭**   **F**
Sing me sweet and sleepy all the way back home.

          Am   **B♭**   **F**
It's a far gone ____ lullaby sung many years a - go.

              G   **B♭**   **F**
Mama, Mama, many worlds I've come since I first left home.

Chorus 2   **F**   **A**
Goin' home, goin' home.

   B♭   **F**   **G**
By the waterside I will rest my bones.

F   **G**
Listen to the river sing ____ sweet songs

 B♭   **F**
To rock my soul.

Verse 3

      F   Bb
Goin' to plant a weeping willow.

                F   Dm   Bb   F
On the bank's ___ green edge it will grow, grow, ___ grow.

              Am   Bb   F
Sing a lullaby ___ be - side the wa - ter.

              G   Bb   F
Lover's come and go; the river roll, roll, roll.

Chorus 3

F   A
Fare you well, fare you well.

Bb   F   G
I love you more than words can tell.

F   G
Listen to the river sing ___ sweet songs

Bb   F
To rock my soul.

Outro

          F   Bb
Do, do, do, ___ do, do, do, do.

F   G   Bb   F
 Do, do, do, do, do, do, do, do.

          Bb   F
Do, do, do, do, do, do, do, do, do.

       G   Bb   F
 Do, do, do, do, do, do, do, do.

       G   Bb   F
Do, do, do, do, do, do, do, do, do.

Bird Song

Words by Robert Hunter
Music by Jerry Garcia

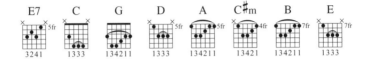

Intro ‖: **E7** | :‖

Verse 1
E7
All I know is, something like a bird within her sang.

All I know, she sang a little while and then flew on.

C G   D   A   E7
Tell me all that you know; I'll ___ show you snow and rain.

Verse 2
E7
If you hear that same sweet song again, will you know why?

Anyone who sings a tune so sweet is passing by.

C   G   D   A   E7
Laugh in the sun - shine, sing, cry in the dark, fly through the night.

| | C#m   B |
| *Chorus 1* | Don't cry now, |

A   E   B
Don't you cry.

A   E   B   A
Don't you cry anymore.

            E
La, la, la, la.

C#m   B
Sleep in the stars,

A   E   B
Don't you cry.

A E   B   A
Dry your eyes on the wind.

            E
La, la, la, la, la, la.

| *Guitar Solo* | ‖: E7 | | | :‖ |

| *Verse 3* | *Repeat Verse 2* |
| *Chorus 2* | *Repeat Chorus 1* |

| *Interlude* | | E7 | | | | |

| *Verse 4* | *Repeat Verse 1* |

| *Outro* | ‖: E7 | | | :‖ *Repeat and fade* |

Black Peter

Words by Robert Hunter
Music by Jerry Garcia

Melody:

All of my __ friends _ come to ____

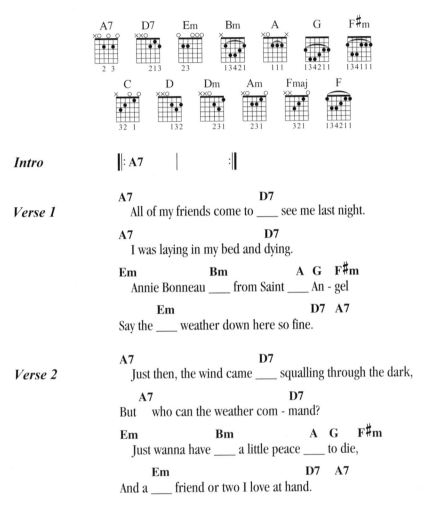

Intro ‖: A7 | :‖

Verse 1
    A7   D7
All of my friends come to ___ see me last night.

    A7   D7
I was laying in my bed and dying.

    Em   Bm   A G F#m
Annie Bonneau ___ from Saint ___ An - gel

         Em   D7 A7
Say the ___ weather down here so fine.

Verse 2
    A7   D7
Just then, the wind came ___ squalling through the dark,

     A7   D7
But   who can the weather com - mand?

    Em   Bm   A G F#m
Just wanna have ___ a little peace ___ to die,

         Em   D7 A7
And a ___ friend or two I love at hand.

Verse 3

A7   D7
Fever roll up to a ___ hundred and five.

A7   D7
Roll on up, gonna roll back down.

Em   Bm   A   G F♯m
One more day ___ I find myself ___ a - live.

  Em   D7
To - morrow, maybe go beneath the ground.

Bridge

 C   D Em
See here, how ev'rything lead up to this day,

Dm   Am   Em
And it's just like any other day that's ___ ever been.

D   G   C Em Am
Sun going up and then the sun going down,

Fmaj7   C   D
Shine through my window, and my friends, they come a - round,

    Dm   F A7
Come a - round, come a - round.

Verse 4

A7   D7
The people might know, but the people don't care

A7   D7
That a man can be as poor as me.

Em   Bm   A G F♯m
Take a look at poor Pe - ter, he's ly - ing in pain.

Em   D7
Now, let's come, run and see, run and see, run and see,

Run, run and see, and see.

Outro   ‖: D7 | :‖

Box of Rain

Words by Robert Hunter
Music by Phil Lesh

Melody:

Look out of an - y win - dow,

A   Asus² / ₄   D   Am   Em   C   G   A7   Bm   A*

1114   1324   132   231   23   32 14   32   4   2 3   13421   111

Intro   ‖: A | Asus²/₄ A | | Asus²/₄ A :‖

Verse 1
D   Am   Em
Look out of an - y window, any morning,

C   G
Any evening, any day.

D   Am   Em
Maybe the sun ___ is shining, birds are winging

G   A7
Or rain is falling from a heavy sky.

Chorus 1
D   G   Am
What do you want ___ me to do, to do for you,

Em   D
To see you through?

C   D
For this is all a dream ___ we dreamed

Am   G
One afternoon long a - go.

Verse 2

```
D              Am            Em
Walk out of an - y doorway, feel your way,

C                          G
Feel your way like the day be - fore.

D              Am            Em
Maybe you'll find direction a - round some corner

    G                      A7
Where it's been waiting to meet ___ you.
```

Chorus 2

```
D          G
What do you want me to do

Am                    Em   D
To watch for you while you're sleep - ing?

    Am                C
Then please don't be surprised

        G              D
When you find ___ me dreaming ___ too.
```

Guitar Solo

```
|G         |        |Am    |Em          |
|C    |A   |D       |      |            |
|G         |        |Am    |Em          |
|G    |D   |Em      |A  Asus²₄ |
|     |A  Asus²₄ |          |
```

Verse 3

```
D              Am   Em
Look into an - y eyes you find by you,

        C              G
You can see clear to another day.

D                  Am
Maybe it's been seen ___ before,

        Em         G              A7
Through other eyes, on other days while going home.
```

                                  D   G
Chorus 3   What do you want ____ me to do,

                          Am   Em   D
                      To do for you, to see you through?

                            C   Em
                      It's all a dream we dreamed

                                  D   G
                      One after - noon long a - go.

                                  D   Am
Verse 4   Walk into splintered sunlight,

                      Em   C   G
                      Inch your way through dead ____ dreams to another land.

                      D   Am
                      Maybe you're tired ____ and broken,

                            Em   G   A7
                      Your tongue is twisted with words half spoken and thoughts unclear.

                                  D   G
Chorus 4   What do you want ____ me to do,

                          Am   Em   D
                      To do for you to see you through?

                          Am   C
                      A box of rain will ease the pain

                            G   D
                      And love will see you through.

```
            G                     Am        Em
Bridge         Just a box of rain, wind and water,

                C                  A
            Be - lieve it if you need ___ it,

                          D
            If you don't ___ just pass it on.

            G                    Am        Em
               Sun and shower, wind and rain,

               G                  D
            In ___ and out the win - dow

                         Em              A   Asus2/4   A   Asus2/4
            Like a moth ___ before a flame.


                     D                Em                  G                  D
Outro       And it's just a box of rain, ___ I don't know ___ who put it there,

                                    Bm              G                 A
            Believe it if you need ___ it, or leave ___ it if you dare.

                     D                  Em         G                   D
            And it's    just a box of rain ___ for a rib - bon for your hair,

                          Em                                         G
            Such a long, ___ long time to be gone and a short ___ time to be there.

            | D    C   | G    D   | A*        |           ||
```

Brown-Eyed Women

Words by Robert Hunter
Music by Jerry Garcia

Melody:

Gone are the days _ when the   ox _ fall _ down, ____

C#m   E   A   B   F#m   Bm   G#m

134111   1333   134211   134211   13421   134111   134111

Intro

| C#m | E | A | |
| 2/4 | 4/4 E | | |

Verse 1

    C#m   E
Gone are the days when the ox fall down,

B   A
Take up the yoke and plow the fields around.

C#m   E
Gone are the days when the ladies said,

      A   E
"Please, gentle Jack Jones, won't you come on to me?"

Chorus 1

               B
Brown-eyed women and red grenadine.

               A   E   B
The bottle was dusty but the liquor was clean.

               A   E   C$\sharp$m
Sound of the thunder with the rain ___ pourin' down,

           F$\sharp$m   A   E
And it looks like the old man's   gettin' on.

Verse 2

               C$\sharp$m   E
Nineteen-twenty when he stepped to the bar.

               B   A
He drank to the dregs of the whiskey jar.

               C$\sharp$m   E
Nineteen-thirty when the wall ___ caved in.

               A   E
He'd make his way sellin' red eye gin.

Chorus 2   *Repeat Chorus 1*

Guitar Solo   ‖: C$\sharp$m |E |B |A |
                   |C$\sharp$m |E |A |$\frac{2}{4}$ |
                   |$\frac{4}{4}$E | :‖ *Play 3 times*

Verse 3

               C$\sharp$m   E
Delilah Jones was the mother of twins

               B   A
Two times over, and the rest ___ were sins.

               C$\sharp$m   E
Raised eight boys, only I turned bad.

               A   E
Didn't get the lickin's that the other ones had.

Chorus 3   *Repeat Chorus 1*

	Bm A E
Bridge	Tumble down shack in Big Foot County,

Bm   **A**   **E**
Snowed so hard that the roof caved in.

C#m   **B**   **A**   **G#m**
Delilah Jones ___ went to meet her God,

       A   **E**
And the old man never was the same a - gain.

Verse 4

     C#m   **E**
     Daddy made whiskey and he made it well.

B   **A**
Cost two dollars and it   burned like hell.

C#m   **E**
I cut hick'ry just to fire the still.

A   **E**
Drink down a bottle and you're ready to kill.

Chorus 4	*Repeat Chorus 1*

Verse 5	*Repeat Verse 1*

Chorus 5

B
Brown-eyed women and red grenadine.

     A   **E**   **B**
The bottle was dusty but the liquor was clean.

A   **E**   **C#m**
Sound of the thunder with the rain ___ pourin' down,

    F#m   **A**   **E**
And it looks like the old man's   gettin' on.

    F#m   **A**   **E**
And it looks like the old man's ___ gettin' on.

Casey Jones

Words by Robert Hunter
Music by Jerry Garcia

Melody:

Driv - in' that train, _ high on co - caine. _

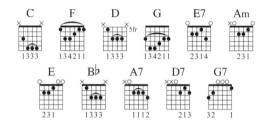

Intro |C   F | C |

Chorus 1

      C   F
Drivin' that train, high on cocaine.

                               C
Casey Jones, you'd better watch your speed.

         F
Trouble ahead, trouble behind.

                           C   F   C
And you know that notion just crossed my mind.

Verse 1

      C   D
This old engine makes it on time.

      F   G
Leaves Central Station 'bout a quarter to nine.

      C   D
Hits River Junction at seventeen to.

              F   E7   Am   G
At a quar - ter to ten ____ you know it's trav'lin' again.

Chorus 2   *Repeat Chorus 1*

Verse 2

```
          C                 D
Trouble ahead, a lady in red.

F                     G
Take my advice you'd be better off dead.

C                      D
Switch man sleeping, train hundred and two

  F          E7      Am        G
Is on the wrong track and headed for you.
```

Chorus 3   *Repeat Chorus 1*

Interlude

```
|C        |D        |F        |G         |
 Oo,       oo,       oo.

|C        |D        |F    E7  |Am  G    |
 Oo,       oo.
```

Guitar Solo   *Repeat Chorus 1 (Instrumental)*

Verse 3

```
        C                    D
Trouble with you is the trou - ble with me.

    F                       G
Got two good eyes but they still ___ don't see,

C                      D
Come 'round the bend you know it's the end.

      F          E       Am        G
The fire - man screams ___ and the engine just gleams.
```

Chorus 4	C F ‖: Drivin' that train, high on cocaine.

                                    C
Casey Jones, you'd better watch your speed.

            F
Trouble ahead, trouble behind.

                                         C
And you know that notion just crossed my mind. :‖

Chorus 5	C B♭ F ‖: Drivin' that train, high ___ on cocaine.

                                  C
Casey Jones, you'd better watch your speed.

        B♭   F
Trouble ahead, trouble behind.

                                     C
And you know that notion just crossed my mind. :‖

A7   D7   G7   C
And you know that notion just crossed my mind.

Candyman

Words by Robert Hunter
Music by Jerry Garcia

Melody:

Come all ___ you pret - ty wom - en,

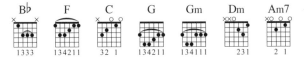

Intro

‖: Bb   F | C   :‖ *Play 4 times*
| G | |

Verse 1

            C   Gm   F
Come all ___ you pretty women, with your hair a hanging down.

                                        G
Open up your windows, 'cause the Candyman's in town.

                    Dm   G   Dm
Come on, boys, and gamble, roll those laughing bones.

F   G
Seven come eleven, boys, I'll take your money home.

Chorus 1

Bb   F   C
Look out, look out, the Candyman,

Bb   F   C
  Here he come and he's gone again.

Am7   G
  Pretty lady ain't got no friend

          F   G
Till the   Candyman comes a - round again.

Verse 2	C Gm F I come in from Memphis, where I learned to talk the jive.

               G
When I get back to Memphis, be one less man alive.

         Dm G   Dm
Good morning, Mister Benson, I see you're doing well.

F   G
If I had me a shotgun, I'd blow you straight to hell.

Chorus 2   *Repeat Chorus 1*

Instrumental *Repeat Verse 1 and Chorus 1 (Instrumental)*

Verse 3	C Gm F Come on, boys, and wager, if you ___ have got the mind.

              G
If you've got a dollar, boys, lay it on the line.

        Dm G   Dm
Hand me my old guitar, pass the whiskey 'round.

F   G
Won't you tell ev'rybody you meet that the Candyman's in town?

Chorus 3	B♭ F C Look out, look out, the Candyman,

B♭   F   C
  Here he come and he's gone again.

Am7   G
  Pretty lady ain't got no friend

       F   G   F C
Till the Candyman comes a - round again.

Outro	B♭ F C ‖: Look out, look out, the Candyman,

B♭   F   C
  Here he come and he's gone again. :‖ *Repeat and fade*

Dire Wolf

Words by Robert Hunter
Music by Jerry Garcia

Melody:

In the tim-bers of Fen - nar - i - o, ___

A   E   D   G   C#7   F#m

Intro | N.C.(A) | E | D | A |

Verse 1
     A   E   G   D
In the timbers of Fennario, the wolves are running 'round.

                                                             E
The winter was so hard and cold, froze ten feet 'neath the ground.

Chorus 1
                D
Don't murder me.

   E   A   C#7   D
   I beg of you, don't murder me.

   E   D   A
   Please, ___ don't murder me.

Verse 2
         E   G   D
I sat down to my supper, was a bottle of red whis - key.

                                             A   F#m
I said my prayers and went to bed, that's the last they saw of me.

GUITAR CHORD SONGBOOK

	E

Chorus 2
                    E
        Don't murder me.

        D   A   D
        I beg of you, don't murder me.

        E   D   A
        Please, ___ don't murder me.

Verse 3
               F#m   E   A   D
        When I ___ awoke the Dire ___ Wolf, six hundred pounds of sin,

                                                  E
        Was grinnin' at my window, all I said was come on in.

Chorus 3
                    D
        But don't murder me.

        E   A   C#7   F#m
        I beg of you, don't murder me.

        E   D   A
        Please, ___ don't murder me.

Verse 4
               F#m   E
        The wolf ___ came in, I got ___ my cards,

               A   G   D
        We sat ___ down for a game.

        I cut my deck to the queen of spades

                            E
        But the cards were all the same.

Chorus 4
                    D
        Don't murder me.

        E   A   C#7   F#m
        I beg of you, don't murder me.

        E   D   A
        Please, ___ don't murder me.

        Don't murder me.

Interlude | F#m | E | A   G | D |
                   | | | | E |
                   | D | E | A   C#7 | F#m |
                   Oo,   oo.
                   | E | D | A | |

                           E   G   D
Verse 5   In the backwash of Fennario, the black and bloody mire.

                                                              E
          The Dire Wolf collects his due while the boys sing 'round the fire.

                           D
Chorus 5   Don't murder me.

          E   A   D
            I beg of you, don't murder me.

          E   D   A
           Please, ___ don't murder me.

                          E
Chorus 6   Don't murder me.

          D   A   C#7   F#m
            I beg of you, don't murder me.

          E   D   A
           Please, ___ don't murder me.

                              E
          No, no, no, don't murder me.

          D   A   C#7   F#m
            I beg of you, don't murder me.

          E   D   A
           Please, ___ don't murder me.

          E   D   A   E   A
          Please, ___ don't murder me.

Franklin's Tower

Words by Robert Hunter
Music by Jerry Garcia and Bill Kreutzmann

Melody:

In an - oth - er time's

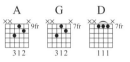

Intro   ‖: A   G │D   G │A   G │D   G :‖

Verse 1
        A   G   D   G
In an - other time's   forgot - ten space,

    A   G   D   G
   Your eyes looked   from your mother's face.

    A   G   D   G
   Wildflower seed ___ on the sand and stone.

    A   G   D   G
   May the four winds blow you safely home.

Chorus 1
    A   G   D G
   Roll away   the dew.

    A   G   D G
   Roll away   the dew.

    A   G   D G
   Roll away   the dew.

    A   G   D G
   Roll away   the dew.

Guitar Solo 1   ‖: A   G │D   G │A   G │D   G :‖

Verse 2

```
   A              G          D           G
I'll  tell you where   the four ___ winds dwell.

A                G              D          G
   In Franklin's tower    there hangs ___ a bell.

A           G    D          G
   It can ring,    turn night to day.

A                  G                D             G
   It can ring like fire when you lose ___ your way.
```

Chorus 2   *Repeat Chorus 1*

Verse 3

```
A                  G           D          G
   God save the child ___ who rings ___ that bell.

A                      G         D              G
   It may have one good ring, baby, you ___ can't tell.

A               G  D             G
   One watch by night,      one watch by day.

A                   G            D            G
   If you get confused, a, listen to the music play.
```

Guitar Solo 2   *Repeat Guitar Solo 1*

Verse 4

```
A                 G           D        G
   Some come to laugh    the past ___ away.

A                 G          D              G
   Some come to make    just one ___ more day.

A            G      D          G
   Whichever way    your pleasure tends,

A              G                 D           G
   If you plant ice, you're gonna har - vest wind.
```

Chorus 3   *Repeat Chorus 1*

Verse 5	A G D G In Franklin's tower the four ___ winds sleep,

A   G   D   G
Like four lean hounds ___ the light - house keep.

A   G   D   G
Wildflower seed in the sand and wind.

A   G   D   G
May the four winds blow you home again.

Chorus 4   *Repeat Chorus 1*

Chorus 5	A G D Roll away the dew.

       G   A   G   D G
You ___ better roll away   the dew.

A   G   D
Roll away   the dew.

G   A   G   D G
You better roll away   the dew.

   A   G   D G
‖: Roll away   the dew.

A   G   D G
Roll away   the dew.   :‖ *Repeat and fade*

Estimated Prophet

Words by John Barlow
Music by Bob Weir

My time com - in' _____ an - y - day; ___

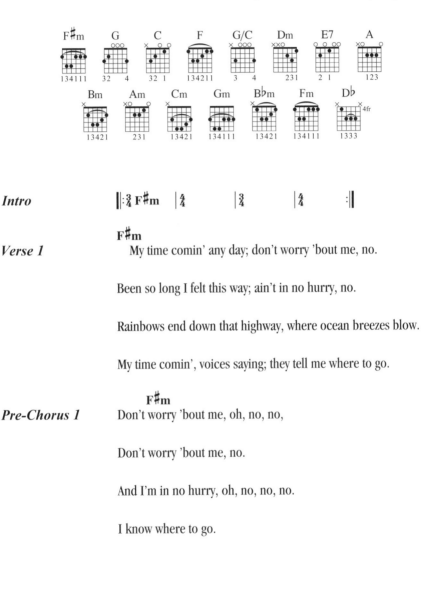

Intro   ‖: ¾ F#m |4/4 |¾ |4/4   :‖

Verse 1
F#m
My time comin' any day; don't worry 'bout me, no.

Been so long I felt this way; ain't in no hurry, no.

Rainbows end down that highway, where ocean breezes blow.

My time comin', voices saying; they tell me where to go.

Pre-Chorus 1
F#m
Don't worry 'bout me, oh, no, no,

Don't worry 'bout me, no.

And I'm in no hurry, oh, no, no, no.

I know where to go.

Chorus 1

         G   C   G
Cali - fornia, preachin' on the burning shore.

F C   G   C   G
    Cali - fornia, I'll be knockin' on the golden door.

F C   G   C   G
    Like an angel standin' in a shaft of light,

F C   G   C   G   F C
    Risin' up to paradise, I know I'm gonna shine.

Verse 2

      F♯m
    My time comin' any day; don't worry 'bout me, no.

It's gonna be just like they say; them voices tell me so.

Seems so long I felt this way, and time sure passin' slow.

Still, I know I lead the way; they tell me where I go.

Pre-Chorus 2   *Repeat Pre-Chorus 1*

Chorus 2

         G   C   G
Cali - fornia, a prophet on the burning shore.

F C   G   C   G
    Cali - fornia, I'll be knockin' on the golden door.

F C   G   C   G
    Like an angel standin' in a shaft of light,

F   C   G   C   G   F C
    And risin' up to paradise, I know I'm gonna shine.

Bridge

G   C   G/C G
You've all been asleep; you would not be - lieve me.

F C   G   C G/C G
    Them voices tellin' me you will soon re - ceive me.

F C   G   C G/C
    We're standin' on the beach; the sea will part be - fore me,

G   F   C
(Fire wheel burning in the air.)

G   C G/C
You will follow me and we will ride to glo - ry.

G   F   C
(Way up the middle of the air.)

Dm   E7
    And I'll call down thunder and speak the same,

Dm   E7
    And my word fills the sky ___ with flame.

Dm   E7
    And might and glory gonna be my name,

Dm
    And men gonna light...

Interlude

| $\frac{3}{4}$ F | | $\frac{4}{4}$ A | | $\frac{3}{4}$ Bm | | $\frac{4}{4}$ Dm | |
My way.

| $\frac{3}{4}$ Am | | $\frac{4}{4}$ Cm | | $\frac{3}{4}$ Gm | | $\frac{4}{4}$ Bbm | |

| $\frac{3}{4}$ Fm | | $\frac{4}{4}$ Db | |

Instrumental	*Repeat Chorus 1 (Instrumental)*

F♯m

Verse 3   My time comin' any day; don't worry 'bout me, no.

It's gonna be just like they say; them voices tell me so.

Seems so long I felt this way, and time sure passin' slow.

My time comin' any day: don't worry 'bout me, no.

F♯m

Outro   Don't worry 'bout me, no, no,

Don't worry 'bout me, no.

‖:And I'm in no hurry, oh, no, no,

Don't worry 'bout me, no. :‖ *Repeat and fade w/ vocal ad lib.*

Eyes of the World

Words by Robert Hunter
Music by Jerry Garcia

Melody:

Right out - side _ this   la - zy _ sum - mer _ home, _

Emaj   A   Bm   A*   C#m   B

A**   D   E   C   G

Intro | Emaj7 | | | |

Verse 1
Emaj7   A   Emaj7   Bm   A*
Right outside this   lazy summer ___ home,

Emaj7   A   Emaj7 Bm   A*
You ain't got time to call your ___ soul a critic,   no.

Pre-Chorus 1
A*   C#m   B   A**
Right outside the lazy gate   of winter's summer home,

C#m   B   D   A**
Wond'rin' where the nuthatch winters,   wings a mile-long

E   A**   E   A**   C
Just   carried the bird a - way.

Chorus 1
G   C   G   C
Wake up to find out that you are the eyes of the world,

G   C   G   C
The heart has its beaches, its homeland and thoughts of its own.

D   C   G   C
Wake now, discover that you are the song that the morning brings,

G
But the heart has its seasons,

C   D   Bm   A*
Its ev'nings and songs of its own.

Guitar Solo 1 ‖: Emaj7 | |Bm | :‖

Verse 2
       Emaj7   **A**
There comes a redeemer and he
                Emaj7 Bm A*
Slowly, too, fades a - way,
       Emaj7   **A**
There follows a wagon be - hind him
               Emaj7 Bm A*
That's loaded with a clay.

Pre-Chorus 2
         A*   **C#m**   **B A****
And the seeds that were silent all burst into bloom and de - cay.
        E   **A****   **E A**** C**
The night comes so quiet, it's close on the heels of the day.

Chorus 2 *Repeat Chorus 1*

Guitar Solo 2 ‖: Emaj7 | |Bm |A* :‖

Verse 3
Emaj7   **A**   **Emaj7 Bm A***
Sometimes we live no par - ticular way but our own,
Emaj7   **A**   **Emaj7 Bm A***
Sometimes we visit your country and live in your home.

Pre-Chorus 3
         A*   **C#m**
Sometimes we ride on your horses,
        B   **A****
Sometimes we walk alone,
        E   **A****
Sometimes the songs that we hear
               E A** C**
Are just songs of our own.

Chorus 3 *Repeat Chorus 1*

**Outro-
Guitar Solo** ‖: Emaj7 | :‖ *Repeat and fade*

Fire on the Mountain

Words by Robert Hunter
Music by Mickey Hart

Melody:

Long dis-tance run - ner what you

B   A

3 2 1 1   3 2 1 1

Intro   ‖: B | |A | :‖

Verse 1

B   A
Long distance runner, what you standin' there for?

B   A
Get up, get out, get out of the door.

B   A
You're playin' cold music on the barroom floor.

B   A
Drowned in your laughter and dead to the core.

B   A
There's a dragon with matches that's loose on the town.

B   A
Takes a whole pail of water just to cool him down.

Chorus 1

         B   A
‖: Fire! Fire on the mountain!

B   A
Fire! Fire on the mountain! :‖

Verse 2	**B** **A** Almost ablaze, still you don't feel the heat.

B   **A**
It takes all you got just to stay on the beat.

B   **A**
You say it's a livin', we all ___ gotta eat.

B   **A**
But you're here alone, there's no one to compete.

B   **A**
If mercy's a business, I wish it for you.

B   **A**
More than just ashes when your dreams come true.

Chorus 2   *Repeat Chorus 1*

Guitar Solo   ‖: B | |A | :‖ *Play 4 times*

Verse 3

B   **A**
Long distance runner, what you holdin' out for?

B   **A**
Caught in slow motion in a dash to the door.

B   **A**
The flame from your stage has now spread to the floor.

B   **A**
You gave all you had, why you wanna give more?

B   **A**
The more that you give the more ___ it will take

B   **A**
To the thin line beyond which you really can't fake.

Outro   *Repeat Chorus 1 and fade*

Friend of the Devil

Words by Robert Hunter
Music by Jerry Garcia and John Dawson

I lit up __ from Re - no, I ___ was

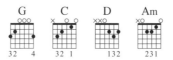

Intro   ‖:G |C |G |C   :‖

Verse 1

G   C
I lit up from Reno, I was trailed by twenty hounds.

G   C
Didn't get to sleep that night 'til the morning came around.

Chorus 1

D
Set out runnin' but I take my time,

   Am
A friend of the Devil is a friend of mine.

D
I get home before daylight,

Am   D
Just might get some sleep to - night.

Verse 2

  G   C
Ran into the Devil, babe, he loaned ___ me twenty bills.

  G   C
Spent the night in Utah, in a cave ___ up in the hills.

Chorus 2   *Repeat Chorus 1*

Verse 3

  G   C
I ran down to the levee, but the Dev - il caught me there.

  G   C
Took my twenty dollar bill and he vanished in the air.

Chorus 3   *Repeat Chorus 1*

Bridge 1

  D
Got two reasons why I cry away each lonely night.

      C
The first one's name's sweet Anne Marie and she's my heart's delight.

  D
Second one is prison, baby, the sheriff's on my trail.

      Am   C   D
And if he catches up with me I'll spend my life in jail.

Verse 4

  G   C
Got a wife in Chino, babe, and a one in Cherokee.

  G   C
First one say she got my child but it don't look like me.

Chorus 4   *Repeat Chorus 1*

Guitar Solo		G		C		G		C	
		D		Am		D		Am	
		D							

Bridge 2

D
Got two reasons why I cry away each lonely night.

    C
The first one's name's sweet Anne Marie and she's my heart's delight.

D
Second one is prison, babe, and the sheriff's on my trail.

   Am   **C**   **D**
And if he catches up with me I'll spend my life in jail.

Verse 5   *Repeat Verse 4*

Chorus 5

   D
I set out runnin' but I take my time,

  Am
A friend of the Devil is a friend of mine.

D
I get home before daylight,

Am   **D**
Just might get some sleep to - night.

He's Gone

Words by Robert Hunter
Music by Jerry Garcia

Melody:

Rat in a drain ditch

E   A   B   Asus4   E7/D   F#m   E*

D   A/C#   B*   A*   G   F

Intro

‖: E | A | E | A :‖

Verse 1

E   A E
Rat in a drain ditch   caught on a limb,

A   B   E   A E   A
You know better but I know him.

E   A E
Like I told you,   what I said,

A   B   E   A E
Steal your face right off your head.

Chorus 1

             A Asus4 E   A Asus4 E
Now he's gone, _____ now he's gone,

E7/D   A   B
Lord, he's gone, he's gone.

         A   B
Like a   steam locomotive, rollin' down the track.

        A   E   E7/D   A
He's gone, gone, nothin's gonna bring him back.

       E   A E A
He's gone.

Verse 2
```
E           A   E
Nine mile skid on a ten mile ride,

A                    B      E   A E    A
Hot as a pistol but cool ___ in - side.

E           A   E
Cat on a tin roof,     dogs in a pile,

A                    B      E        A E
Nothin' left to do but smile, ___ smile, smile.
```

Chorus 2   *Repeat Chorus 1*

Interlude
```
|F#m    |        |E      |        |
|F#m    |        |E*   D |A/C#    |
|       |E       |       |        |       |
```

Guitar Solo   *Repeat Verse 1 (Instrumental)*

Bridge
```
B*              D              A*
  Goin' where the wind don't blow so strange,

B*                   D              A*
  Maybe off on some high cold mountain chain.

D               A*      G
Lost one round but the price wasn't anything,

D        F       A       B
A knife in the back and more of the same.
```

Verse 3

              E   A E
Same old rat in a drain ditch,   caught on a limb,

A   B   E   A
You know better but I know him.

E   A E
Like I told you,   what I said,

A   B   E
Steal your face right off your head.

Chorus 3

          A Asus4 E   A Asus4 E
Now he's gone, _____ now he's gone,

E7/D   A   B
Lord, he's gone, he's gone.

     A   B
Like a   steam locomotive, rollin' down the track.

     A   E   E7/D   A
He's gone, gone, nothin's gonna bring him back.

    E   A E
He's gone.

     A   B
Like a   steam locomotive, rollin' down the track.

     A   E   E7/D   A
He's gone, gone, nothin's gonna bring him back.

    E   A E   A E
He's gone.

Outro

    E
‖: Oo, nothin's gonna bring him back. :‖ ***Repeat and fade***
                                         w/ vocal ad lib.

The Golden Road

Words and Music by Jerry Garcia,
Bill Kreutzmann, Phil Lesh,
Ron McKernan and Bob Weir

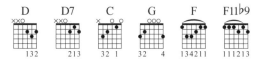

Intro | D | | | D7 |

Verse 1

D   C
See that girl barefootin' a - long?

G   D
Whistlin' and singin', she's a carryin' on.

                                    C
Got laughin' in her eyes, dancin' in her feet.

            F   C
She's a neon light diamond.

          G   D
She can live on the street.

Chorus 1

            D   C
Hey, hey, ____ come right a - way.

G   D
Come and join the party every day.

                     C
Hey, hey, come right a - way.

G   D
Come and join the party every day.

Verse 2	**D** **C** Ev'rybody's dancin' in a ring around the sun.

D   **C**
Ev'rybody's dancin' in a ring around the sun.

G   **D**
Nobody's finished, we ain't even be - gun.

                                                C
So take off your shoes, child, and take off your hat.

F   **C**   **G**   **D**
Try on your wings and find out where it's at.

Chorus 2   *Repeat Chorus 1*

Guitar Solo   ‖: **D** | **C** | **G** | **D**   :‖ *Play 3 times*

Verse 3   **D**   **C**
Take a vacation, fall out for a while.

G   **D**
Summer's comin' in and it's goin' out - ta style.

                                           C
Well, lie down smokin', honey, have yourself a ball,

                        F   **C**   **G**   **D**
'Cause your mother's down in Memphis, won't be back 'til the fall.

Chorus 3   **D**   **C**
‖: Hey, hey, ___ come right a - way.

G   **D**
Come and join the party every day.

                               C
Hey, hey, come right a - way.

G   **D**
Come and join the party every day. :‖

Outro | **D** | | **F11♭9** ‖

High Time

Words by Robert Hunter
Music by Jerry Garcia

You told me good - bye. _____

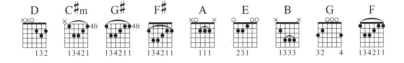

D   C#m   G#   F#   A   E   B   G   F

Verse 1

>   D   C#m
> You told me good - bye.
>
> G#   F#   A   E
> How was I to know   you didn't mean good - bye?
>
> D   A
> You meant please ____ don't let me go.
>
>   B   E
> I was having a high time,
>
> B A   E
>   Living the good life.
>
> D   A   E   G A
> Ah, ____ well, I know.

Verse 2

>   D   C#m G#   F#
> The wheels are muddy,   got a ton of hay.
>
> A   E   D   A
>   Now, listen here, baby,   'cause I mean what I say.
>
>   B   E
> I'm havin' a hard time
>
> B A   E
>   Livin' the good life.
>
> D   A   E   G
> Ah, ____well, I know.

                          F
Bridge   I was losing time.

                   E   B
                   I had nothing to do, no one to fight

                C#m A E
                I came to you.

                   F   E
                   Wheels broke down, the leader won't draw

                      B   C#m   A E
                   The line is busted, the last one I   saw.

                |D | |A | |

                        A N.C. D   C#m   G#   F#
Verse 3   To - morrow come trouble,   tomorrow come pain.

                   A   E
                   Now, don't think too hard, baby,

                   D   A
                   'Cause you know what I'm sayin'.

                           B   E
                   I could show you a high time,

                   B A   E
                         Livin' the good life.

                   D   A   E   G A
                   Ah, ___ don't be that way.

                        D   C#m   G#   F#
Verse 4   Nothing's for certain,   it could always go wrong.

                   A   E   D   A
                   Come in when it's raining,   go on out when it's gone.

                            B   E
                   We could have us a high time,

                   B A   E
                         Living the good life.

                   D   A   E
                   Ah, ___ well, I know.

I Know You Rider

Traditional
Arranged by Jerry Garcia, Keith Godchaux,
William Kreutzmann, Phil Lesh,
Ronald McKernan and Bob Weir

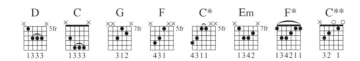

Intro   ‖: D | | :‖ ***Play 4 times***

Chorus 1

      D   C   G   D
I know you, rider, gonna miss me when I'm gone.
                        C   G   D
I know you, rider, gonna miss me when I'm gone.
      F   C*   F   C* Em D
Gonna miss your baby from rolling in   your arms.

Verse 1

      D   C   G   D
Laid down last night, Lord, I could not take my rest.
                        C   G   D
Laid down last night, Lord, I could not take my rest.
      F   C*   F   C* Em D
My mind was wand'ring like the wild geese in the west.

Guitar Solo 1   *Repeat Verse 1 (Instrumental)*

Verse 2

```
            D              C        G         D
The sun will shine in my back - yard some - day.
                        C        G         D
The sun will shine in my back - yard some - day.
          F       C*    F    C*   Em    D
March winds will blow all my trou - bles a - way.
```

Verse 3

```
            D                    C     G        D
I wish I was a headlight    on a northbound ___ train.
                           C        G      D
I wish I was a headlight ___ on a north - bound train.
F         C*                F           C* Em  D
I'd shine my light through the    cool Colo - ra - do   rain.
```

Chorus 2   *Repeat Chorus 1*

Guitar Solo 2   *Repeat Verse 1 (Instrumental)*

Chorus 3

```
N.C.
I know you rider, gonna miss me when I'm gone.
```

I know you rider, gonna miss me when I'm gone.

Gonna miss your baby from rolling in your arms.

Outro

```
|F*      |C**     |F*      |C** Em  |
|D       |        |        |        ‖
```

(Walk Me Out in The) Morning Dew

Words and Music by
Bonnie Dobson and Tim Rose

Melody:

Walk me out ___ in the morn-ing dew, ___

D   C   G   C*   Em/B

132   1333   134211   32 1   12

Intro

‖: 4/4 D | C G | D | 2/4 :‖
| 4/4 D | C G | D | C G |

Verse 1

    D   C   G   D
Walk me out in the mornin' dew, my honey.

                  C   G   D
Walk me out in the mornin' dew, to - day.

F   C*   Em/B D
Can't walk you out in the the mornin' dew, my honey.

F   C*   Em/B D   C G
I can't walk you out in the morning dew, to - day.

Verse 2

    D   C   G   D
I thought I heard a baby cry this mornin'.

               C   G   D
I thought I heard a baby cry to - day.

F   C*   Em/B D
You didn't hear no ___ baby cry this morning.

F   C*   Em/B D   C F D C G
You didn't hear no ___ baby cry to - day.

Verse 3

```
          D                    C          G      D
          Where have all the people gone, ___ my honey?

                        C     G     D
          Where have all the people gone to - day?

               F
          Well,    there's no need for you to be

          C*          Em/B        D
          Worryin' about ___ all those people.

          F                        C*  Em/B D    C G
          You never see those peo - ple any  -  way.
```

Verse 4

```
          D                    C          G      D
          I thought I heard a young man born this morning.

                          C          G      D
          I thought I heard a young man born to - day.

          F                C*          Em/B    D
          I thought I heard a young man born this morning.

          F                         C*           Em/B    D
          I can't walk you out in the morning dew ___ to - day.
```

Guitar Solo   *Repeat Verse 1 (Instrumental)*

Verse 5

```
          D                    C     G      D
          Walk me out in the mornin' dew, my honey.

                         C     G      D
          Walk me out in the mornin' dew, to - day.

          F                    C*      Em/B   D
          I'll walk you out in the morning dew, my honey.

          F               C*       Em/B  D
          I guess it doesn't matter any - way.

                  F            C*    Em/B    D
          Well, I    guess it doesn't matter ___ any - way.

          F               C*       Em/B  D
          I guess it doesn't matter any - way.     ***Fade out***
```

New Speedway Boogie

Words by Robert Hunter
Music by Jerry Garcia

Melody:

Please _ don't dom-i-nate the rap, Jack,

E7   G   D   A

Intro | E7 | | | |

Verse 1
       E7
Please don't dominate the rap, Jack, if you got nothing new to say.

If you please, don't back up the track, this train's got to run today.

I spent a little time on the mountain, spent a little time on the hill.
                                           G   **D**   **A**
I heard some say, "Better run away." Oth - ers say, "Better stand still."
      E7
Now, I don't know, but I've been told
      G   **D**   **A**
It's hard ___ to run ___ with the weight of gold.
E7
Other hand, I heard it said,
      G   **D**   **A**   **E7**
It's just ___ as hard ___ with the weight of lead.

Verse 2

E7
Who ___ can deny, who can deny it's not just a change in style?

One step done and another begun, and I wonder how many miles.

I spent a little time on the mountain, spent a little time on the hill.

                                                      G   D   A
Things went down we don't understand, but I think ___ in time we will.

        E7
Now, I ___ don't know, but I was told

     G   D   A
In the heat of the sun ___ a man died of cold.

E7
Keep on coming, or stand and wait,

              G   D   A   E7
With the sun ___ so dark and the hour so late.

Verse 3

     E7
You ___ can't overlook the lack, Jack, of any other highway to ride.

It's got no signs or dividing lines, and very few rules to guide.

I spent a little time on the mountain, I spent a little time on the hill.

                                            G   D   A
I saw things getting' out of hand, I guess ___ they always will.

     E7
Now, I don't know, but I've been told

     G   D   A
If the horse don't pull, you got to carry the load.

E7   G   D   A
I don't know whose back's that strong, maybe find out be - fore too long.

Outro

     E7
‖: One way or another, one way or another,

One way or another, this darkness got to give. :‖ *Repeat and fade*

Ramble On Rose

Words by Robert Hunter
Music by Jerry Garcia

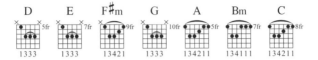

Melody:

Just like Jack the Rip - per,

D   E   F#m   G   A   Bm   C

Intro   ‖: D | | | :‖

Verse 1
D   E
Just like Jack the Ripper, just like Mojo Hand.

F#m   G   D   G   A
Just like Billy Sun - day   in a shotgun ragtime band.

D   E
Just like New York City, just like Jericho.

F#m   G   D
Pace the halls and climb the walls,

                 G   A
And get out ___ when they blow.

Chorus 1
D   G
  Did you say your name was   Ramblin' Rose?

E   G   D
  Ramble on, baby,   settle down easy.

A   D
  Ramble on, Rose.

Verse 2

D	E

Just like Jack and Jill,　　Poppa told the jailer.

F#m　　　　　**G**　　　　**D**
One heat up and one cool down,

　　　　　　　　　G　　　**A**
Leave nothing for the tail - or.

D　　　　　　　　　**E**
Just like Jack and Jill, Momma told the sailor.

F#m　　**G**　　　**D**
One go up, one go down.

　　　　　　　　　G　　　**A**
Do yourself ___ a fa - vor.

Chorus 2　　　*Repeat Chorus 1*

Bridge 1

Bm　　　　　　　　**C**
I'm gonna sing you　　a hundred versus of ragtime.

Bm　　　　　　　　　　**C**　　　　**G**
I know this song, it ain't　　never gonna end.

Bm　　　　　　　　　　　　**C**
I'm gonna march you up and down　　the local county line.

D　　　　　　　　**A**　　　　**Bm**　**E**　**A**
Take you to the lead - er of the band.

Guitar Solo

‖: D　　　｜E　　　｜F#m　G D ｜2/4　　G　｜

｜4/4 A　　｜D　　　｜E　　　　｜F#m　G D ｜

｜2/4　G　｜4/4 A　:‖

｜D　　　｜E　　　｜F#m　G D ｜2/4　　G　｜

｜4/4 A　　｜

Verse 3

    D   E
Just like Crazy Otto, just like Wolfman Jack.

F♯m   G D   G   A
  Sittin' plush with a roy - al flush, aces back to back.

    D   E
Just like Mary Shelley, just like Frankenstein.

F♯m   G   D
Break your chains and count your change

          G   A
And try to walk the line.

Chorus 3   *Repeat Chorus 1*

Bridge 2

Bm   C
  I'm gonna sing you   a hundred versus of ragtime.

Bm   C   G
  I know this song, it ain't   never gonna end.

Bm   C
  I'm gonna march you up and down   the local county line.

D   A   Bm E A
  Take you to the lead - er of the band.

Verse 4

    D   E
Goodbye Momma and Poppa, goodbye Jack and Jill.

    F♯m   G   D
The grass ain't greener, the wine ain't sweet - er,

          G   A
Either side ___ of the hill. ___ Oh.

Chorus 4

D   G
  Did you say your name was   Ramblin' Rose?

E   G   D
  Ramble on, baby,   settle down easy.

A   D   A   D
  Ramble on, Rose.   Ramble on, Rose.

Rosemary

Words by Robert Hunter
Music by Jerry Garcia

Melody:

Boots were of leath - er, a

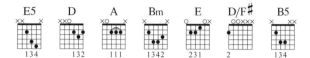

E5   D   A   Bm   E   D/F#   B5

Verse 1

    E5   **D**
Boots were of leather, a breath of cologne.

    A   **Bm**   **A**   **E**
Her mirror was a window she sat by a - lone.

                D/F#
All under, around her, the garden grew,

    A   **Bm**   **A**   **B5**
Scarlet and purple and crimson and blue.

Verse 2

    E5   **D**
She came and she went, and at last went away.

    A   **Bm**   **A**   **E**
The garden was sealed when the flowers de - cayed.

                D/F#
On the wall of the garden, a legend did say,

    A   **Bm**   **A**   **B5**
No one may come here since no one may stay.

Outro

Repeat Verse 1 (Instrumental) and fade

Ripple

Words by Robert Hunter
Music by Jerry Garcia

Melody:

If my words did glow __

G   C   D   Am   A

Intro

G		C		
			G	
		C		
G	D	C	G	

Verse 1

   G   C
If my words did glow with the gold of ___ sunshine,
                                      G
And my tunes were played on the harp, unstrung,
                           C
Would you hear my voice come through the music?
                G   D C   G
Would you hold ___ it near, ___ as if it were your own?

Verse 2

                  G   C
It's a hand me down, ___ the thoughts are ___ broken.
                      G
Perhaps they're better left un - sung.
                  C
I don't know, don't really care.
G   D C   G
Let there be songs ___ to fill the air.

Chorus 1

Am   D
Ripple in still water,
                 G   C
When there is ___ no pebble tossed.
      A   D
No wind to blow.

Verse 3

                                  G   C
Reach out your hand, ___ if your cup be ___ empty.

                             G
If your cup is full, may it be again.

                       C
Let it be known, there is a fountain

G   D C   G
That was not made ___ by the hands of man.

Verse 4

                          G   C
There is a road, ___ no simple ___ highway,

                                G
Between the dawn and the dark of night.

                           C
And if you go, no one may ___ follow.

G   D C   G
That path is for ___   your steps alone.

Chorus 2   *Repeat Chorus 1*

Verse 5

                          G   C
You who choose ___ to lead must ___ follow.

                             G
But if you fall, you fall alone.

                             C
If you should stand, then who's to ___ guide you?

G   D C   G
If I knew the way, I would take you home.

Outro

                          G   C
La, n, da, da, da. ___ La, da, da, da, da.

                             G
Da, da, da, da, da, da, da, da, da, da.

                           C
La, n, da, da, da. La, da, da, da, da.

G   D C   G
La, da, da. ___ La, da, da, da, da.

Scarlet Begonias

Words by Robert Hunter
Music by Jerry Garcia

As I was walk - in' 'round Gros-ve-nor Square, _

B   E   A   F#

3 2 1 1   1 3 3 3   3 2 1 1   3 2 1 1

Intro   ‖: B | | | :‖

Verse 1
       E   B
As I was walkin' 'round Grosvenor Square,

  A   E   B
Not a chill to the winter but a nip to the air.

  A   E   B A   E
From the other di - rec - tion she was calling my eye.

  A   E B A   E   B
It could be an illu - sion, but I might as well try, might as well try.

Verse 2
       E   B
She had rings on her fingers and bells on her shoes,

  A   E   B
And I knew ___ without askin' she was into the blues.

  A   E   B A   E
She wore scarlet be - go - nias   tucked into her curls.

  A   E B   A   E   B
I knew right a - way she was not like the other girls, other girls.

Verse 3   E   B

In the thick of the evening the dealing got rough,

                           A   E   B

She was too ___ pat to open and too cool to bluff.

                           A   E   B A   E

As I picked up my match - es   and was closing the door,

                           A   E   B

I had one of those flash - es,

                           A   E   B

I'd been there be - fore, been there be - fore.

Bridge   F$\sharp$

Well, I ain't often right, but I've never been wrong.

                           B   A   E

Seldom turns out the way it does in the song.

                           F$\sharp$

Once in a while, you get shown the light

                              B   A

In the strangest of places if you look at it…

Interlude | E | | F$\sharp$ | |

                       Right.

                  | A | | B | |

                  | | |

Verse 4
                        E   B
Well, there ain't nothin' wrong with the way she moves,

           A   E   B
Or scarlet begonias or a touch of the blues.

           A   E   B   A   E
And there's nothin' wrong with the look ___ that's in her eye.

           A   E   B A   E   B
I had to learn the hard way   to let her pass by, let her pass by.

Guitar Solo   *Repeat Verse 1 (Instrumental)*

Verse 5
                         E   B
The wind in the willows playin' "Tea for Two,"

           A   E   B
The sky was yellow and the sun was blue.

           A   E   B   A   E
Strangers stoppin' stran - gers just ___ to shake their hand.

           A   E   B A   E   B
Ev'rybody is play - ing   in the heart of gold band, heart of gold band.

Outro   ‖: B | | | :‖ ***Repeat and fade***

Ship of Fools

Words by Robert Hunter
Music by Jerry Garcia

Melody:

Went to see the cap - tain, _____

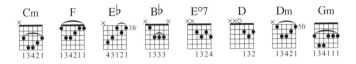

Intro |Cm |F |E♭ |B♭ |

Verse 1

B♭   F   E♭
Went to see the cap - tain,

E°7   B♭
Strangest I could find.

          D   E♭
Laid my ___ propo - sition down,

Cm   F
Laid it on the line.

           E♭   B♭
I won't slave for beggar's pay,

Dm   Cm
Likewise gold and jewels.

E♭   B♭
But I would slave to learn the way

F   E♭   B♭
To sink your ___ ship of fools.

Chorus 1

     F   **E♭** **B♭**
Ship of fools on a cruel sea.

     F   **E♭** **Gm**
Ship of fools, sail a - way from me.

            E°7
It was later than I thought when I first believed you.

    Cm   **F**   **E♭**   **B♭**
Now I cannot share your laughter, ___ ship of fools.

Verse 2

B♭   **F**   **E♭**
 Saw your first ship sink ___ and drown

E°7   **B♭**
 From rockin' of the boat.

       D   **E♭**
And all that ___ could not sink or swim

Cm   **F**
 Was just left there to float.

      E♭   **B♭**
I won't leave you driftin' down,

Dm   **Cm**
 But, whoa, it makes me wild,

E♭   **B♭**
 With thirty years up - on my head,

   F   **E♭**   **B♭**
To have you ___ call me "child."

Chorus 2   *Repeat Chorus 1*

Verse 3

B♭   F E♭
The bottles stand as emp - ty

E°7   B♭
As they were filled be - fore.

         D   E♭
Time there ____ was, and plenty,

Cm   F
But from that cup no more.

        E♭   B♭
Though I could not caution all,

Dm   Cm
I still might warn a few.

E♭   B♭
Don't lend your hand to raise no flag

 F   E♭   B♭
A - top no ____ ship of fools.

Chorus 3

       F   E♭ B♭
Ship of fools on a cruel sea.

       F   E♭   Gm
Ship of fools, sail a - way from me.

         E°7
It was later than I thought when I first believed you.

     Cm   F   E♭   B♭
Now I cannot share your laughter, ____ ship of fools.

     Gm   E°7
It was later than I thought when I first believed you.

     Cm   F   E♭   B♭
Now I cannot share your laughter, ____ ship of fools.

Outro-Guitar Solo   *Repeat Verse 1 (Instrumental) and fade*

Sugar Magnolia

Words by Robert Hunter
Music by Bob Weir

Melody:

Su - gar mag - no - lia,

A   D   E   G   C#m   F#m   B   E*   F#

111   312   231   3211   1342   13111   111   312   3211

Intro

A		D A		
		D A		E A
		E A		

Verse 1

        A   D   A
Sugar magnolia, blossoms bloom - ing

            G   E   A
Heads all empty and I don't care.

           C#m   F#m
Saw my baby down by the river,

  E   D   A E A
Knew she had to come up soon for air.

Verse 2

        A   D   A
Sweet blossom come on, under the wil - low.

           G   E   A
We can have high times if you'll abide.

           C#m   F#m
We can discover the wonders of nature,

  E   D   A   E A
Rolling in the rushes, down by the riverside.

Chorus 1

```
D            G          D
She's got ev'ry - thing delight - ful.

            A     D
She's got ev'ry - thing I need.

                    G          D
Takes the wheel when I'm ___ seeing double.

            E       A      E    A
Pays my ticket    when I speed.
```

Interlude

```
|A        |  D  A |      E |    A  |
|         |  D  A |        |E   A  |
|         |E  A  |
```

Verse 3

```
A                                      D   A
    Well, she comes skimming through rays of vi - 'let.

      G     E      A
She can wade in a drop of dew.

                    C♯m  F♯m
She don't come and I don't follow.

E                   D      A  E  A
Waits backstage while I sing to you.
```

Verse 4

```
A                  D     A
    Well, she can dance a Cajun rhythm,

            G   E         A
Jump like a Wil - lys in four wheel drive.

                    C♯m          F♯m
She's a summer love in the spring, fall and winter.

E                  D        A  E  A
She can make happy,    any man a - live.
```

Bridge

```
          A      G    D  A
Sugar magno - lia,

          G       D  A
Ringing that bluebell.

              G     D  A
Caught up in the sun - light.

          E        G            D
Go on out singin' I'll walk you in the sunshine.

                       A     E  A
Oo, come on honey, come along with me.
```

Chorus 2

```
D              G          D
She's got ev'ry - thing delight - ful.

          A     D
She's got ev'ry - thing I need.

                   G        D
A breeze in the pines in the summer night moonlight.

                   E         A   E  A
Crazy in the sunlight, ___ yes indeed.
```

Verse 5

```
A                            D   A
  A sometimes when the cuckoo's cry - ing,

           D      A
When the moon is halfway down.

B                 E*    B
  Sometimes when the night is dying,

              F♯       E*   D  A  E*
I take me out and I wander a - round.

B          A     E*  B
  I wander 'round.
```

Verse 5

```
‖: B              |    E* B E*  |
  (Do, do, do,    do, do, do, do.

| B        F♯ |    E          :‖ Repeat and fade
  Do, do, do, do,   do, do, do.)    w/ lead vocal ad lib.
```

Tennessee Jed

Words by Robert Hunter
Music by Jerry Garcia

Melody:

Cold iron   shack-les and ball _____   and chain. _

C   G   F   G*   C*   C7   C°7   Bb

3211   1333   134211   134211   1333   1314   2314   1333

Intro

C	G C			
	G C			
	G C		G C

Verse 1

        C   G C
Cold iron shackles and ball and chain.

F   G*   C*   C G C
Listen to the whistle of the evenin' train.

C7   C°7   F   C7
   Well, you know ____ you bound to   wind up dead,

        F   G*   C*   C G C
You don't head back to Ten - nessee, Jed.

Verse 2

        C   G C
Rich man step on my poor head.

F   G*   C*   C G C
When you get back, you better butter my bread.

C7   C°7   F   C7
   Well, you know ____ people,   it's a like I said,

        F   G*   C* Bb F G* C*
You better head back to Ten - nessee, Jed.

Chorus 1

        F
Tennessee, Tennessee,

        C*   **G***   **F**
There ain't no place I'd ___ rather be.

C*   **G*** **F**
Baby, won't you carry me

C*   **G***   **F**   **G* C***
Back to ___ Tennessee.

Interlude 1

‖: C | | | G C |

| | | | G C |

| | G   C :‖

Verse 3

C   **G C**
Drinked all day and rocked all night.

     F   **G***   **C***   **C G C**
The law come to get you if you don't walk right.

C7   **C°7**   **F**   **C7**
   Got a letter this morn - in', people,   all it read

     F   **G***   **C***   **C G C**
"You better head back to Tennessee, Jed."

Verse 4

  C   **G C**
I dropped four flights and cracked my spine.

F   **G*** **C*** **C G C**
Honey, come quick with the iodine.

C7   **C°7**   **F**   **C7**
   Gonna catch a few ___ winks, baby,   under the bed.

F   **G***   **C*** **B♭ F G* C***
Then you head back to Ten - nessee, Jed.

Chorus 2   *Repeat Chorus 1*

Interlude 2

‖: C | | | G   C :‖

| | G C |

Verse 5

```
         C              G  C
         I run into Charlie Fog.

         F              G*        C*  C  G  C
         Blacked my eye and he kicked my dog.

         C7      C°7        F       C7
          My doggie    turned to me and he said,

          F              G*      C*    C  G  C
         "Let's head back to Ten - nessee, Jed."
```

Verse 6

```
         C                       G  C
         I woke up a feelin' mean.

         F                    G*        C*  C  G  C
         Went down to play the slot ___ machine.

         C7                C°7        F                C7
          The wheels turned a - round people,    and the letters read,

           F              G*      C*  F G* C*
         "You better head back to Ten - nessee, Jed."
```

Chorus 3   *Repeat Chorus 1*

Guitar Solo

```
‖: C      |        |         | G   C  :‖ Play 4 times
‖: F      |        |         |        :‖
‖: G*     |        |         |        :‖
‖: C      |        |         | G   C  :‖ Play 4 times
‖: F      |        |         |        :‖
 | G*     |        |         |         |
 |        |        | B♭  F   | G*  C*  |
```

Chorus 4

```
         F
         Tennessee, Tennessee,

            C*             G*          F
         There ain't no place I'd ___ rather be.

         C*          G*  F
         Baby, won't you carry me

         C*      G*         F    G* C* B♭ F G* C*
         Back to ___ Tennessee.
```

Touch of Grey

Words by Robert Hunter
Music by Jerry Garcia

Melody:

It must be get - ting ear - ly, ___

A   E   B   F#   C#m   C#   G#m   D#7   C#7   D#

Intro

N.C.	A	E	A	E	B	F#	B
F#	A	E	A	E	B	F#	B
F#	A	E	A	E	B	F#	B
F#		

Verse 1

    B   F# B
It must be getting ear - ly,

E   A E
Clocks are running late,

F#   B
Paint by number morning sky,

E
Look so phony.

B   F#   B
Dawn is breaking ev - 'rywhere,

E   A   E
Light a candle, curse ___ the glare,

F#   B
Draw the curtains, I don't care,

      E
'Cause   it's alright.

Chorus 1

F# B   E
I will get by,

F# B   E
I will get by,

F# B   A E
I will get by,

F#   E   A E   B F#   B F#
I will survive.

Verse 2

B   F#   B
I see you've got your fist ___ out,

E   A   E
Say your piece and get ___ out,

F#   B
Yes, I get the gist of it,

    E
But   it's alright.

B   F#   B
Sorry that you feel ___ that way,

E   A   E
The only thing there is ___ to say,

F#   B   E
Ev'ry silver lining's got ___ a   touch of grey.

Chorus 2

Repeat Chorus 1 (Instrumental)

Bridge 1

C#m   C#   F#
It's a les - son to me,

   C#m   C#   F#
The Ables and the Bak - ers and the C's.

G#m   D#7 C#7   F#
The ABC's ___   we all must face,

B   E   F#
Try to keep ___ a little grace.

Guitar Solo

Repeat Verse 1 & Chorus 1 (Instrumental)

Bridge 2

C#m   C#   F#
It's a les - son to me,

C#m   C#   F#
The Deltas and the East ____ and the freeze.

G#m   D# C#   F#
The ABC's ____ we all think of

B   E   F#
And try to win ____ a little love.

Verse 3

B   F#   B
I know the rent is in ____ arrears,

E   A   E
The dog has not been fed ____ in years

F#   B
It's even worse than it appears,

     E
But   it's alright.

B   F#   B
Cow is givin' ker - osene,

E   A   E
Kid can't read at sev - enteen,

F#   B
The words he knows are all ob - scene,

     E
But   it's alright.

Chorus 3   *Repeat Chorus 1*

Verse 4

B   F#   B
The shoe is on the hand ___ it fits,

E   A   E
There's really nothing much ___ to it,

F#   B
Whistle through your teeth and spit

       E
'Cause   it's alright.

B   F#   B
Oh, well, a touch ___ of grey

E   A   E
Kinda suits you any - way,

F#   B
And that was all I had to say

       E
And   it's alright.

Chorus 4

F# B   E
I will get by,

F# B   E
I will get by,

F# B   A E
I will get by,

F#   E A E B F# B F#
I will survive.

Chorus 5

     F#   B   E
‖: We will get by,

F#   B   E
We will get by,

F#   B   A E
We will get by,

F#   E A E B F# B F#
We will survive.   :‖ *Repeat and fade*

Truckin'

Words by Robert Hunter
Music by Jerry Garcia,
Phil Lesh and Bob Weir

Melody:

Truck - in',   got __ my chips cashed _ in, ___

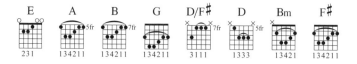

E	A	B	G	D/F♯	D	Bm	F♯
231	134211	134211	134211	3111	1333	13421	134211

Intro   ‖: E | | :‖

Chorus 1
        E
Truckin', got my chips cashed in,

        A
Keep truckin', like the doo-dah man.

        B
To - gether, more or less in line.

    A   E
Just keep truckin' on.

Verse 1
        E
Arrows of neon and flashing marquees out on Main Street.

Chicago, New York, Detroit and it's all on the same street.

Your typical city involved in a typical day dream,

Hang it up and see what tomorrow brings.

Chorus 2	E Dallas got a soft machine.
	A Houston, too close to New Orleans.
	B New York got the ways and means
	A E But just won't let you be.

Verse 2

E
What in the world ever became of Sweet Jane?

She lost her sparkle, you know she isn't the same.

Living on reds, vitamin C and cocaine,

All a friend can say is ain't it a shame.

Chorus 3

E
Truckin', off to Buffalo,

    A
Been thinkin' you got to mellow slow.

B
Takes time to pick a place to go,

    A   E
And just keep truckin' on.

	E
Verse 3	You're sick of hanging around and you'd like to travel,

Get tired of traveling, you want to settle down.

I guess they can't revoke your soul for try'n'.

Get out of the door, light out and look all around.

	A G D/F♯ A
Bridge	Sometimes the light's all shining on me.

                                    D   A   G D/F♯ A
Other times I can barely see.

D   Bm   F♯
Lately it oc - curs to me

Bm F♯   A   E
    What a long, strange trip it's been.

	E
Chorus 4	Truckin', I'm a, going home.

A
Whoa, whoa, baby, back where I belong.

B
Back home, sit down and patch my bones

    A   E
And get back truckin' on.

Outro	‖: E │ │ │ :‖ *Repeat and fade*

Uncle John's Band

Words by Robert Hunter
Music by Jerry Garcia

Well, the first days _ are _ the hard-est days, _

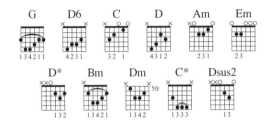

Intro

| G | | | | |
| D6 C | D | G D6 C | D | |

Verse 1

        G
Well, the first days are the hardest days,

       C   G
Don't you worry an - ymore.

'Cause when life looks like easy street

       C   G
There is danger at your door.

Am   Em
Think this through with me,

C   D*
Let me know your mind.

C   D*   G   D* C G
Whoa, oh, what I want to know

   D*   G
Is are you kind?

Verse 2

       G
It's a buck dancer's choice my friends,

      C   G
Better take my advice.

You know all the rules by now,

      C   G
And the fire from the ice.

Am   **Em**
Will you come with me?

C   **D***
Won't you come with me?

C **D***   **G**   **D*** **C** **G**
Whoa, oh, what I want to know,

   D*   **G**
Will you come with me?

Pre-Chorus 1

G   **C**
 God damn, well, I declare,

Am   **Em**   **D***
Have you seen the like?

     C
Their walls are built of cannonballs;

    G **D***   **C**   **D***
Their motto is "Don't tread on me."

Chorus 1

G   **C**
Come hear Uncle John's band

Am **G** **D***
Playing to the tide.

C
Come with me or go alone,

    G **D***   **C**   **D***
He's come to take his children home.

| Interlude 1 | |G D6 C | D |G Bm C | D | |
| | |G Bm C | D |G Bm C | D | |

Verse 3

      G
It's ___ the same story the crow told me,

     C   G
It's the only one he knows.

Like the morning sun you come,

     C   G
And like the wind you go.

Am   **Em** **C**   **D***
Ain't no time to hate; ___ barely time to wait.

C   **D***   **G**   **D* C G**
Whoa, oh, what I want to know,

      D*   **G**
Where does the time go?

Verse 4

      G
  I live in a silver mine,

     C   G
And I call it Beg - gar's Tomb.

                C   G
I got me a violin, and I beg you call the tune.

Am   **Em** **C**   **D***
Anybody's choice, ___ I can hear your voice.

C   **D***   **G**   **D* C G**
Whoa, oh, what I want to know,

      D*   **G**
How does the song go?

Chorus 2

<pre>G   C</pre>
Come hear Uncle John's band

<pre>Am   G   D*</pre>
By the river - side.

<pre>C</pre>
Got some things to talk about,

<pre>G   D*   C   D*</pre>
Here, beside the rising tide.

<pre>G   C</pre>
Come hear Uncle John's band

<pre>Am   G   D*</pre>
Playing to the tide.

<pre>C</pre>
Come on along or go alone,

<pre>   G   D*   C   D*</pre>
He's come to take his children home.

Interlude 2

‖: $\frac{4}{4}$ Dm | $\frac{3}{4}$ G   C*   :‖   *Play 7 times*
| $\frac{4}{4}$ Dm | |

Dm
Whoa, oh, what I want to know,

<pre>C   G</pre>
How does the song go?

Chorus 3	N.C. Come hear Uncle John's band by the riverside. Got some things to talk about, Here, beside the rising tide. G C Come hear Uncle John's band Am G D* Playing to the tide. C Come on along or go alone, G D* C D* He's come to take his children home.

Outro	$\left|\frac{4}{4}\right.$Dm |
	$\left|\frac{3}{4}\right.$G C* $\left|\frac{4}{4}\right.$Dm |
	  Da, da, da, da, da, da.
	$\left|\frac{3}{4}\right.$G C* $\left|\frac{4}{4}\right.$Dm |
	  Da, da, da, da, da, da.
	$\left|\frac{3}{4}\right.$G C* $\left|\frac{4}{4}\right.$Dsus2 ‖
	  Da, da, da, da, da, da.

Guitar Chord Songbooks

Each book includes complete lyrics, chord symbols, and guitar chord diagrams.

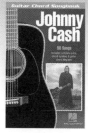

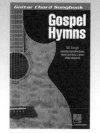
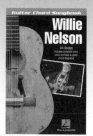

Acoustic Hits
More than 60 songs: Against the Wind • Name • One • Southern Cross • Take Me Home, Country Roads • Teardrops on My Guitar • Who'll Stop the Rain • Ziggy Stardust • and more.
00701787 ....$14.99

Acoustic Rock
80 acoustic favorites: Blackbird • Blowin' in the Wind • Layla • Maggie May • Me and Julio down by the Schoolyard • Pink Houses • and more.
00699540..............................$21.99

Alabama
50 of Alabama's best: Angels Among Us • The Closer You Get • If You're Gonna Play in Texas (You Gotta Have a Fiddle in the Band) • Mountain Music • When We Make Love • and more.
00699914..............................$14.95

The Beach Boys
59 favorites: California Girls • Don't Worry Baby • Fun, Fun, Fun • Good Vibrations • Help Me Rhonda • Wouldn't It Be Nice • dozens more!
00699566..............................$19.99

The Beatles
100 more Beatles hits: Lady Madonna • Let It Be • Ob-La-Di, Ob-La-Da • Paperback Writer • Revolution • Twist and Shout • When I'm Sixty-Four • and more.
00699562..............................$17.99

Bluegrass
Over 40 classics: Blue Moon of Kentucky • Foggy Mountain Top • High on a Mountain Top • Keep on the Sunny Side • Wabash Cannonball • The Wreck of the Old '97 • and more.
00702585..............................$14.99

Johnny Cash
58 Cash classics: A Boy Named Sue • Cry, Cry, Cry • Daddy Sang Bass • Folsom Prison Blues • I Walk the Line • Ring of Fire • Solitary Man • and more.
00699648..............................$17.99

Children's Songs
70 songs for kids: Alphabet Song • Bingo • The Candy Man • Eensy Weensy Spider • Puff the Magic Dragon • Twinkle, Twinkle Little Star • and more.
00699539..............................$16.99

Christmas Carols
80 Christmas carols: Angels We Have Heard on High • The Holly and the Ivy • I Saw Three Ships • Joy to the World • O Holy Night • and more.
00699536..............................$12.99

Christmas Songs
80 songs: All I Want for Christmas Is My Two Front Teeth • Baby, It's Cold Outside • Jingle Bell Rock • Mistletoe and Holly • Sleigh Ride • and more.
00119911..............................$14.99

Eric Clapton
75 of Slowhand's finest: I Shot the Sheriff • Knockin' on Heaven's Door • Layla • Strange Brew • Tears in Heaven • Wonderful Tonight • and more.
00699567 ....$19.99

Classic Rock
80 rock essentials: Beast of Burden • Cat Scratch Fever • Hot Blooded • Money • Rhiannon • Sweet Emotion • Walk on the Wild Side • and more.
00699598 ....$18.99

Coffeehouse Hits
57 singer-songwriter hits: Don't Know Why • Hallelujah • Meet Virginia • Steal My Kisses • Torn • Wonderwall • You Learn • and more.
00703318 ....$14.99

Country
80 country standards: Boot Scootin' Boogie • Crazy • Hey, Good Lookin' • Sixteen Tons • Through the Years • Your Cheatin' Heart • and more.
00699534 ....$17.99

Country Favorites
Over 60 songs: Achy Breaky Heart (Don't Tell My Heart) • Brand New Man • Gone Country • The Long Black Veil • Make the World Go Away • and more.
00700609 ....$14.99

Country Hits
40 classics: As Good As I Once Was • Before He Cheats • Cruise • Follow Your Arrow • God Gave Me You • The House That Built Me • Just a Kiss • Making Memories of Us • Need You Now • Your Man • and more.
00140859 ....$14.99

Country Standards
60 songs: By the Time I Get to Phoenix • El Paso • The Gambler • I Fall to Pieces • Jolene • King of the Road • Put Your Hand in the Hand • A Rainy Night in Georgia • and more.
00700608 ....$12.95

Cowboy Songs
Over 60 tunes: Back in the Saddle Again • Happy Trails • Home on the Range • Streets of Laredo • The Yellow Rose of Texas • and more.
00699636 ....$19.99

Creedence Clearwater Revival
34 CCR classics: Bad Moon Rising • Born on the Bayou • Down on the Corner • Fortunate Son • Up Around the Bend • and more.
00701786 ....$16.99

Jim Croce
37 tunes: Bad, Bad Leroy Brown • I Got a Name • I'll Have to Say I Love You in a Song • Operator (That's Not the Way It Feels) • Photographs and Memories • Time in a Bottle • You Don't Mess Around with Jim • and many more.
00148087 ....$14.99

Complete contents listings available online at www.halleonard.com

Crosby, Stills & Nash
37 hits: Chicago • Dark Star • Deja Vu • Marrakesh Express • Our House • Southern Cross • Suite: Judy Blue Eyes • Teach Your Children • and more.
00701609............................$16.99

John Denver
50 favorites: Annie's Song • Leaving on a Jet Plane • Rocky Mountain High • Take Me Home, Country Roads • Thank God I'm a Country Boy • and more.
02501697 ....$17.99

Neil Diamond
50 songs: America • Cherry, Cherry • Cracklin' Rosie • Forever in Blue Jeans • I Am...I Said • Love on the Rocks • Song Sung Blue • Sweet Caroline • and dozens more!
00700606 ....$19.99

Disney
56 super Disney songs: Be Our Guest • Friend like Me • Hakuna Matata • It's a Small World • Under the Sea • A Whole New World • Zip-A-Dee-Doo-Dah • and more.
00701071 ....$17.99

The Doors
60 classics from the Doors: Break on Through to the Other Side • Hello, I Love You (Won't You Tell Me Your Name?) • Light My Fire • Love Her Madly • Riders on the Storm • Touch Me • and more.
00699888 ....$17.99

Eagles
40 familiar songs: Already Gone • Best of My Love • Desperado • Hotel California • Life in the Fast Lane • Peaceful Easy Feeling • Witchy Woman • more.
00122917 ....$16.99

Early Rock
80 classics: All I Have to Do Is Dream • Big Girls Don't Cry • Fever • Itsy Bitsy Teenie Weenie Yellow Polkadot Bikini • Let's Twist Again • Lollipop • and more.
00699916 ....$14.99

Folk Pop Rock
80 songs: American Pie • Dust in the Wind • Me and Bobby McGee • Somebody to Love • Time in a Bottle • and more.
00699651 ....$17.99

Folksongs
80 folk favorites: Aura Lee • Camptown Races • Danny Boy • Man of Constant Sorrow • Nobody Knows the Trouble I've Seen • and more.
00699541 ....$14.99

40 Easy Strumming Songs
Features 40 songs: Cat's in the Cradle • Daughter • Hey, Soul Sister • Homeward Bound • Take It Easy • Wild Horses • and more.
00115972 ....$16.99

Four Chord Songs
40 hit songs: Blowin' in the Wind • I Saw Her Standing There • Should I Stay or Should I Go • Stand by Me • Turn the Page • Wonderful Tonight • and more.
00701611 ....$14.99

Glee
50+ hits: Bad Romance • Beautiful • Dancing with Myself • Don't Stop Believin' • Imagine • Rehab • Teenage Dream • True Colors • and dozens more.
00702501 ....$14.99

Gospel Hymns
80 hymns: Amazing Grace • Give Me That Old Time Religion • I Love to Tell the Story • Shall We Gather at the River? • Wondrous Love • and more.
00700463 ....$14.99

Grand Ole Opry®
80 great songs: Abilene • Act Naturally • Country Boy • Crazy • Friends in Low Places • He Stopped Loving Her Today • Wings of a Dove • dozens more!
00699885 ....$16.95

Grateful Dead
30 favorites: Casey Jones • Friend of the Devil • High Time • Ramble on Rose • Ripple • Rosemary • Sugar Magnolia • Truckin' • Uncle John's Band • more.
00139461 ....$14.99

Green Day
34 faves: American Idiot • Basket Case • Boulevard of Broken Dreams • Good Riddance (Time of Your Life) • 21 Guns • Wake Me Up When September Ends • When I Come Around • and more.
00103074 ....$14.99

Irish Songs
45 Irish favorites: Danny Boy • Girl I Left Behind Me • Harrigan • I'll Tell Me Ma • The Irish Rover • My Wild Irish Rose • When Irish Eyes Are Smiling • and more!
00701044 ....$14.99

Michael Jackson
27 songs: Bad • Beat It • Billie Jean • Black or White (Rap Version) • Don't Stop 'Til You Get Enough • The Girl Is Mine • Man in the Mirror • Rock with You • Smooth Criminal • Thriller • more.
00137847 ....$14.99

Billy Joel
60 Billy Joel favorites: • It's Still Rock and Roll to Me • The Longest Time • Piano Man • She's Always a Woman • Uptown Girl • We Didn't Start the Fire • You May Be Right • and more.
00699632 ....$19.99

Elton John
60 songs: Bennie and the Jets • Candle in the Wind • Crocodile Rock • Goodbye Yellow Brick Road • Sad Songs Say So Much • Tiny Dancer • Your Song • more.
00699732 ....$15.99

Ray LaMontagne
20 songs: Empty • Gossip in the Grain • Hold You in My Arms • I Still Care for You • Jolene • Trouble • You Are the Best Thing • and more.
00130337............................$12.99

Latin Songs
60 favorites: Bésame Mucho (Kiss Me Much) • The Girl from Ipanema (Garôta De Ipanema) • The Look of Love • So Nice (Summer Samba) • and more.
00700973 ....$14.99

Love Songs
65 romantic ditties: Baby, I'm-A Want You • Fields of Gold • Here, There and Everywhere • Let's Stay Together • Never My Love • The Way We Were • more!
00701043............................$14.99

Bob Marley
36 songs: Buffalo Soldier • Get up Stand Up • I Shot the Sheriff • Is This Love • No Woman No Cry • One Love • Redemption Song • and more.
00701704............................$17.99

Bruno Mars
15 hits: Count on Me • Grenade • If I Knew • Just the Way You Are • The Lazy Song • Locked Out of Heaven • Marry You • Treasure • When I Was Your Man • and more.
00125332 ....$12.99

Paul McCartney
60 from Sir Paul: Band on the Run • Jet • Let 'Em In • Maybe I'm Amazed • No More Lonely Nights • Say Say Say • Take It Away • With a Little Luck • and more!
00385035 ....$16.95

Steve Miller
33 hits: Dance Dance Dance • Jet Airliner • The Joker • Jungle Love • Rock'n Me • Serenade from the Stars • Swingtown • Take the Money and Run • and more.
00701146............................$12.99

Modern Worship
80 modern worship favorites: All Because of Jesus • Amazed • Everlasting God • Happy Day • I Am Free • Jesus Messiah • and more.
00701801 ....$16.99

Motown
60 Motown masterpieces: ABC • Baby I Need Your Lovin' • I'll Be There • Stop! In the Name of Love • You Can't Hurry Love • and more.
00699734 ....$17.99

Willie Nelson
44 favorites: Always on My Mind • Beer for My Horses • Blue Skies • Georgia on My Mind • Help Me Make It Through the Night • On the Road Again • Whiskey River • and many more.
00148273 ....$17.99

Nirvana
40 songs: About a Girl • Come as You Are • Heart Shaped Box • The Man Who Sold the World • Smells like Teen Spirit • You Know You're Right • and more.
00699762 ....$16.99

Roy Orbison
38 songs: Blue Bayou • Oh, Pretty Woman • Only the Lonely (Know the Way I Feel) • Working for the Man • You Got It • and more.
00699752 ....$17.99

Peter, Paul & Mary
43 favorites: If I Had a Hammer (The Hammer Song) • Leaving on a Jet Plane • Puff the Magic Dragon • This Land Is Your Land • and more.
00103013 ....$19.99

Tom Petty
American Girl • Breakdown • Don't Do Me like That • Free Fallin' • Here Comes My Girl • Into the Great Wide Open • Mary Jane's Last Dance • Refugee • Runnin' Down a Dream • The Waiting • and more.
00699883 ....$15.99

Pink Floyd
30 songs: Another Brick in the Wall, Part 2 • Brain Damage • Breathe • Comfortably Numb • Hey You • Money • Mother • Run like Hell • Us and Them • Wish You Were Here • Young Lust • and many more.
00139116 ....$14.99

Pop/Rock
80 chart hits: Against All Odds • Come Sail Away • Every Breath You Take • Hurts So Good • Kokomo • More Than Words • Smooth • Summer of '69 • and more.
00699538 ....$16.99

Praise and Worship
80 favorites: Agnus Dei • He Is Exalted • I Could Sing of Your Love Forever • Lord, I Lift Your Name on High • More Precious Than Silver • Open the Eyes of My Heart • Shine, Jesus, Shine • and more.
00699634 ....$14.99

Elvis Presley
60 hits: All Shook Up • Blue Suede Shoes • Can't Help Falling in Love • Heartbreak Hotel • Hound Dog • Jailhouse Rock • Suspicious Minds • Viva Las Vegas • and more.
00699633 ....$17.99

Queen
40 hits: Bohemian Rhapsody • Crazy Little Thing Called Love • Fat Bottomed Girls • Killer Queen • Tie Your Mother Down • Under Pressure • You're My Best Friend • and more!
00702395 ....$14.99

Red Hot Chili Peppers
50 hits: Californication • Give It Away • Higher Ground • Love Rollercoaster • Scar Tissue • Suck My Kiss • Under the Bridge • and more.
00699710 ....$19.99

The Rolling Stones
35 hits: Angie • Beast of Burden • Fool to Cry • Happy • It's Only Rock 'N' Roll (But I Like It) • Miss You • Not Fade Away • Respectable • Rocks Off • Start Me Up • Time Is on My Side • Tumbling Dice • Waiting on a Friend • and more.
00137716 ....$17.99

Bob Seger
41 favorites: Against the Wind • Hollywood Nights • Katmandu • Like a Rock • Night Moves • Old Time Rock & Roll • You'll Accomp'ny Me • and more!
00701147 ....$12.99

Carly Simon
Nearly 40 classic hits, including: Anticipation • Haven't Got Time for the Pain • Jesse • Let the River Run • Nobody Does It Better • You're So Vain • and more.
00121011 ....$14.99

Sting
50 favorites from Sting and the Police: Don't Stand So Close to Me • Every Breath You Take • Fields of Gold • King of Pain • Message in a Bottle • Roxanne • and more.
00699921 ....$17.99

Taylor Swift
40 tunes: Back to December • Bad Blood • Blank Space • Fearless • Fifteen • I Knew You Were Trouble • Look What You Made Me Do • Love Story • Mean • Shake It Off • Speak Now • Wildest Dreams • and many more.
00263755 ....$16.99

Three Chord Acoustic Songs
30 acoustic songs: All Apologies • Blowin' in the Wind • Hold My Hand • Just the Way You Are • Ring of Fire • Shelter from the Storm • This Land Is Your Land • and more.
00123860 ....$14.99

Three Chord Songs
65 includes: All Right Now • La Bamba • Lay Down Sally • Mony, Mony • Rock Around the Clock • Rock This Town • Werewolves of London • You Are My Sunshine • and more.
00699720 ....$17.99

Two-Chord Songs
Nearly 60 songs: ABC • Brick House • Eleanor Rigby • Fever • Paperback Writer • Ramblin' Man Tulsa Time • When Love Comes to Town • and more.
00119236 ....$16.99

U2
40 U2 songs: Beautiful Day • Mysterious Ways • New Year's Day • One • Sunday Bloody Sunday • Walk On • Where the Streets Have No Name • With or Without You • and more.
00137744 ....$14.99

Hank Williams
68 classics: Cold, Cold Heart • Hey, Good Lookin' • Honky Tonk Blues • I'm a Long Gone Daddy • Jambalaya (On the Bayou) • Your Cheatin' Heart • and more.
00700607 ....$16.99

Stevie Wonder
40 of Stevie's best: For Once in My Life • Higher Ground • Isn't She Lovely • My Cherie Amour • Sir Duke • Superstition • Uptight (Everything's Alright) • Yester-Me, Yester-You, Yesterday • and more!
00120862 ....$14.99

HAL•LEONARD®

Prices, contents and availability subject to change without notice.

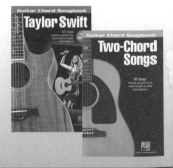

Complete contents listings available online at www.halleonard.com